United Artists

Publication of this book was supported by a grant from the
Eric Mathieu King Fund of The Academy of American Poets.

THE
James
DICKEY
CONTEMPORARY POETRY SERIES

EDITED BY RICHARD HOWARD

United Artists

Poems by S. X. Rosenstock

1996

UNIVERSITY OF SOUTH CAROLINA PRESS

Published in Columbia, South Carolina, by the
University of South Carolina Press

Manufactured in the United States of America

00 99 98 97 96   5 4 3 2 1

Library of Congress Cataloging-in-Publication Data

Rosenstock, S. X.
    United Artists : poems / by S. X. Rosenstock.
        p.   cm. — (James Dickey contemporary poetry series)
    ISBN 1–57003–130–4. — ISBN 1–57003–131–2 (pbk. : alk. paper)
    I. Title. II. Series.
PS3568.08362U55 1996
811' .54—dc20   95–53351

for Coco Owen

Dürer would have seen a reason for living . . .

—Marianne Moore

Contents

A Note on S. X. Rosenstock

To make free with culture is perhaps the last action of Eros to be exploited by a member of our society—certainly the last behavior to be looked for from a poet. (Our escutcheoned poets, nowadays, are culture-*bound,* and it is that bondage, that mansuetude, which secures, even when it scares, their poetry at all.) Yet such *making free* is just the conduct of Ms. Rosenstock, a new and startling poet not so much in our midst as on our margins, our outskirts, as it were, to be noted, to be identified, and to be saluted with a certain hilarity. She is at liberty— she *takes* the liberty— to move among the monuments, and among the ruins, with a strange (to my ears) insouciance (she is not insolent about the masters, except perhaps in the case of "acceptable feminine behavior"), and the consequence of her movements, these poems, are surely the most affectionately aimed spitballs ever lobbed into the courts of High Culture.

Her specific pleasure, even more than her stories, her *imaginary lives,* surely, is the business of syntax, overheard sentences braided over and under the grammatical hurdles like a sort of technicolor wickerwork, though it is just these jumps over the barricades that she takes so handsomely, so gleefully. Her delight in the preposterous, the unavailing, the not-to-be-cloned is apparent from the inside out; her diction, her tropes, her allusions all tend to carve up the funeral baked meats (Coole Park) into designer hors d'oeuvres (Coole Jerk)! Wharton and Plath, like Mme Bovary's daughter and Pauline de Rothschild's decorator, are prodded into patterns wickedly subservient to Rosenstock's will. Hers is a will to challenge (more than to change), and what it challenges are certain patriarchal codes revealed by her experience to be . . . uncertain. Pleasure does not always mean pleasing men.

These are evidently poems written to beguile Rosenstock's ear *first,* before canonical considerations flatten out the silly or sorry sublimities into sensible ones. Like Florine Stettheimer (whom she resembles in her palette and her impasto), this poet is unconcerned to *mind,* as Nurse used to say. She wants, in her eager, trusting way, to *matter,* and caresses the gorgeous syllables, the odd words, the amazing references, the forced temperatures, until she does. On the way, she wants you to have a good time, even a redeemed one, but if not, not. That one doesn't do it? Try this. As Nurse would say: Did you ever?

If there is any Advice to the Reader which might be offered on the threshold of this glistening echo-chamber of imaginative utterances, it is to abandon all anxiety of allusion-catching here. It will be even more fun if you can guess who Marcel might be, if you will bother to look up the Marschallin or (Lord help us!) Ray Bradbury. But not before you let the poems work their cooing, buzzing, garrulous way into your innocent ears.

The Thesaurus of Pleasure welcomes a new work within its narrow purlieus: to Ms. Rosenstock arms are extended from such *doyens* as Valery Larbaud, Daisy Ashford, Raoul Dufy, and, breathless with adoration,

Richard Howard

Acknowledgments

Grateful acknowledgment is made to these publications in which the following poems first appeared:

The Paris Review:
Aubrey Beardsley on the Subject of His Own Willful Ignorance of the *Caprichos* of Francisco Goya

Le Réalisme Fantastique de Berthe Bovary Lipschitz en Anglais Américain

Western Humanities Review:
Doyenne du Comice

Pretext

The Women of *Jekyll & Hyde*

    The author thanks Judith Hall for her great kindness.

    Special thanks to Susan Gorton, Edward Hirsch, John Hollander, Ana Estela Villavicencio, Stephen Yenser, and to Jean and Richard Solomon and the gang at the old Marjan's Deli for welcoming the writing and rewriting of poetry at their restaurant.

    The author's deepest thanks of all are given here, with love, to Richard Rosenstock and to Alison Blythe Rosenstock.

    To one Bernard Salteena-Hyssops, (Lord! I grow purple at the lie; no, I was purple always.) an author offers *countless cakes besides also ices jelly merangs jam tarts with plenty of jam on each some cold tongue some ham with salid and a pig's head done up in a wondrous manner* as evidence of her abiding and sumshious friendsheep.

United Artists

Plath

It's happened at last. Booties
With besom insets have accrued
To my acuity. Mucklucks with birch
And hazel broomlets malaprop
My sense of the bootless. They fit

My feet to perfection. I'm fitted to
Perfection like I'm the very last.
There are no ties. No ties at all.
OK, the tongue ties, but looks dumb.
Look, little brushy besoms fly

The flat parabola between
Boot and boot (me) around the sky.
I'm on my back, and wish for booty
Gloves, mits with sweeping fringe.
I'd make a quadruped; I'd do

If I had extremities covered,
Had a completing yew, a handle
On flying circles all around
Wit shocked literal. It was wearing,
Wasn't it, the death of make-believe?

Close Your Eyes and Think of England

I. Affective Vision

A gavage has crashed my chance at manhood
By being me turning on a toilet,
Bleary and doubling back, imperiled near
The flat cache I, aching, am and ape, a

Sack of one eye, grafted paint in a sort
Of gouge, and a remove, a remove of
Paint.

for Francis Bacon

II. Ego Orgasm

I haven't lost myself to cerebration;
My history comes with me as I think
The world of the world, and my body isn't gone.
I haven't lost myself to cerebration:
My body's come: I am someone alone:
I am accomplished zeal. (It's my instinct.)
I haven't lost myself to cerebration.
My history comes with me as I think.

for D.W. Winnicott

III. The Only Pretty Ring Time

Assent now, softly, to the promises
I make you in an English not to trust.
It's started wars, bought, sold, recorded, kept
Them up, then traded them for peaces more
Wept at than war.
                        I'm carrying the corpse,
My previous addresses, in a lump
My throat is carrying, and carrying
A tune: *It is a lover and his lass . . .*
The tongue admits epithalamion!

                                        for Helen Mirren

3

Aubrey Beardsley on the Subject
of His Own Willful Ignorance
of the *Caprichos* of Francisco Goya

No one misunderstands my satieties
Once he has had at the *Caprichos*
Without knowing what they are, that they are,
That Goya existed.
                          I do rest my long face on sheets
Of paper and the spirits of *the thing to be*
Release themselves into a kind of massage of me
That so incites and embarrasses my self-possession,
I draw
      —kings, queens; the designs are not preordained—
                                                      them out
As I have been found, drawn, out.
It *is* ordained that I sleep with my work
Ruined by my sleeping hacking.

Goya had Spanish ladies
Sit upon and —it can't be said otherwise—smudge,—
Sincerely!—*smudge* the living daylights
Out of his work. Chiaroscuro
Results from women making a tuffet of somebody's cartoon.

The diapering of natural children is done
Of cartoons which are later laundered
In a tincture of tears and set out
On a line near which a small boy is
Assigned the task of crying out, "Dry. As far as I can discern,
And I am a lonely, misused boy with no dog,
They're bloody well dry."

In my bones and in my sidesplitting
Lungs, I am not
Like other men; rather, I contain
A skeleton that is a liquid,
A brine, whippet-mix, a *real, artful* one.
It teethes on my work,
Evidence of which I try
To hide in some lines of a nervy
Opacity: I am exhumed
In ignorance.

Señor Goya permitted cosies
Made of his cartoons; I know.
And the milkmaid was forever
Lining her pail with his satires, and then hanging
Them out to dry in the merciless
Spanish midday sun where they would rot
Open some invective in their mildew
That spoke reams to the painter, and they would
Have to be both salvaged and redone.

When I was three I dreamed I was bleeding
Into the *Caprichos.* I dreamed I was not so much
Satiric as young. I bled a baby onto a pasty.
I kept fainting and fainting into vividness
In the dream. England was wordless and night
Was falling when I was three and I worked
Like a dog in the ensuing years to be
Ignorant of the *Caprichos,* in the dark
And perfectly clear.

Of All of Literature,
Art, Philosophy, Politics & Cuisine
Now or Ever

Dwarf *toreros* on the Champs Élysées;

Dwarf *toreros* on any High Street;

Dwarf *toreros* at the Rose Bowl at halftime;

Dwarf *toreros* at a swearing-in, one sporting
A catechism atop the eight sombreros, the whole
Of his troupe's holdings in hats, which he wears stacked,
Lineatures, over his rough, clean, red hair;

Two teenaged dwarf *toreros*, nonidentical twins, as the front
And hind ends respectively of a mock *caballo* moving
With all the grace of your Aunt Mildred's laden
Cardtable if it could gain an engine and a shot
At an afternoon on the lunar
Surface;
         Polished, professional twin dwarf *toreros*, well-hidden
And prepared now, lightly padded and prepared
For their dwarf-topped encounter here and now
In Bogotá with a *toro* the size of the city
Of El Monte, California, *E.U. de A.*

Eight dwarf *toreros* fighting "El Monte!"

One crack group of six dwarf *toreros* moving at breakneck
Speed atop their hardworking brethren and yet able
To discriminate their mass
Into specialized wings of two dwarf *picadores*
And two dwarf *banderilleros* servicing
One free-floating clown and one prime
Matador;

One neometaphysical dwarf *torero* in charge, scarlet indeed, brash,
Well-spoken, nearly thirty, wielding a double-edged
Something imported from *España* and taking
Umbrage at the characterization of one of his
Co-workers as "a free-floating clown";

Say, one of the wide world's dwarf Boteros is revealed
To be a woman of twenty-one, a bottle
Blonde with about three months' worth of roots,
And four months pregnant,
Glowing, looking forward
To some time off, flying
Through the air off the shoulders of the two calm
Picadores with perfectly bent knees which absorb
The shock of the vigorous running of the two dwarf
Toreros playing the part
Of the horse, steady as they go, as
Serene a platform as any from which to hurl
Oneself expertly into the dulcet and not only South American sky
While chiding, "*Está bien, Félix,*
La verdad es que yo soy una free-
floating clown."

for Fernando Botero

The Women of *Jekyll & Hyde*

The beef cubes bob in broth
I cool with whistling breath

as I walk from room to room,
a stainless spoon, for you,

clenched in my teeth. You're wet
with tears and chilling sweat,

half up, half down, on the couch.
I hand you soup and touch

the spread of white chenille,
so careful not to spill

a drop, as I prop, and fluff,
and wrap you warm enough

to make childhood uncold.
I'm seven years, and odd.

You glance at the TV;
I turn it on and see

young Lana Turner: sex:
I whistle at her breasts

and earn your grin: there's more:
"Wow, Bergman as the whore,

inspired casting, Dad."
What's pleased you gets you mad.

I wash the stained white spread
with Salvo: what I said

caused you to dump, with a jerk,
your meal, my morning's work,

but preciosity
can't win your emnity;

I know you're thinking of
a woman's free, free love.

The Imaginary Portraits of Simonetta Vespucci

I.

The *Orpheus* was to be had with food,
And in a room with paintings redolent
Of food, the colors stains. And this was good,

This food-adduced confusion of the sense
Of poetry with what appends the mouth
As its content, the tongue's experience

With sweetmeats, speech, and love. (Without a doubt
The synesthesia it was dreaming of,
The nineteenth century.) I've been without

A body since the murder, but the gloves
Of consciousness and time handed my life
This strange evagination of its loves:

The death-surviving-arts: not Marco's wife,
I'm Death's, and Poetry's, and Paint's, and Lust's;
I screamed into a painting like a knife . . . .

They strangled me with ribands from the joust ... ...
The searing screams opened a line in a scene,
The Joust, I'd painted to recall the dust

That clouded Giulio's black hair. I mean
To say my death entered that painting and
Incisively, then gloves like some obscene

Protuberances shot out without hands.
You cannot picture this? The gloves, Time, Mind,
Pulled me into the picture of the man

I'd painted to remember, to define.
I'm just pulverulence on his fine curls
And appetite for bodies, his and mine;

I'm you, my death's, my art's, purlieus; I'm worlds:
You haven't lived until you haven't lived
To call five centuries one fair-haired girl's.

II.

We'd have these suppers often and we'd give
An entertainment of some kind each time,
A play, a crush of sonnets, narratives

Of Greeked Christian philosophy, *bouts-rimés*.
They ate the dates from my sterling epergne,
But my other offerings comprised a crime

For seven guests who were not pleased to learn
INITIATION AT EPIDAUROS
As I presented it. I did discern

The evening's course arouse an animus
That culminated in illustrative
Mayhem, the pith which has made me a ghost

For these five hundred years. I guess I gave
The earth to clergy and aristocrats
And magistrates and mistresses who clearly crave

The sort of underworld that is not that.
The *Orpheus* that's to be had *is* food,
And they need it for their art, that is, the state.

III.

I commence a version of my presentation of the Initiation:

Ten years of training and I misconstrued
Initiation's method and its purpose
When I was dropped into the labyrinth nude

And ever so well prepared if quite nervous
That April day. The earth's gaped mouth was wide,
Then filled by a massive rock with a painted surface

I could not read once I was trapped inside
Darkness sealed off by prayer or peroration.
They swore they'd let me out after nine nights.

It was twenty feet from where I kneeled alone
Up to the ceiling art. They'd pulled their rope.
They'd walked away. I could feel that they were gone.

I rose and walked down the dark steep slope;
My eyes gleaning just what obscurity is,
Pure whimsy with my pulse for its gyroscope.

I managed a trance to charm my cowardice:
I changed my mind as art's trained me to do.
This labyrinth is six parallels. Turn right.

I turned right quick but there was no way through
The solid rock. I put my cheek to the wall.
There's firewood. And provisions. Blankets too.

In a cul de sac near the fifth parallel.
I was provided for! I ran unfearing,
Then stepped into a few thousand snakes, and hell.

IV.

What was the floor is more & porous
  Ripped slip-throughs
    Of the whipping
  Aftershocks of snakes
Pouring through the vortices they are.

Walls, & what was the luxury of oxygen,
  Scale, fully, chill, with a monumentality
    Of icy movement; I'm body deep
  In a failure to be
Cold-blooded.

Fool partitive hate gone, I beg full participation:
  Everything I am must cease
    To ridicule my environment.
  The caul of a useless humanity
Must dilate me out of it.

I—NOW!—annul the most cruel, hysteresial
  Inflexibility, my doom, my life.
    Encompassed separateness, turn caduceus: enforce a reticular
  Vivacity as you die
Animal.

It's temperate, the bestial hieratical,
A changling system, eternal
& only intermittently reptile.
I can tune in human news from the outside: someone's died;
I've six days more.
I'm swathed in blankets, eating dates from a bowl marked
For Our Hierodule.

V.

I've many creature comforts in this clearing,
The cave's fifth emanation of cessation,
A honey pie, dried fruits, seeds, an endearing

Crude basket filled with grain, the pure libation
Of well water, & of course I have my fire
In an odd clay mound that eats the asphyxiation

Of its own smoke. The snakes do not desire
To enter here unless I beg them to,
& I do. We spend two days, then they inspire

A phantasm I will be forced to view:
There is another person in this cave.
Not this, I chide my hissing retinue,

As I seek & find a cliff, a plane, a grave
Surrounded on three sides by smooth rock walls.
Above the hole, a bier's flaunting a wave

Of overstitched white lace which has caught & trawls
To nothingness a body which is mine.
I don't seem old or sad, & I sport a shawl

Appliqué'd with emblems, ermine, a vine.
I am to wear this on the final day,
& I'm to make pictures to pass the time.

On the first rock wall I'm moved to paint displays
Of art supplies. On the next two walls I paint
The backs of heads in a crowd & I enchase

Each head with art supplies, brushes, pens, tint, . . .
This gains me prophecies: *Man's love must fail!*
You'll have a baby girl! There's more . . . but I faint.

VI.

In some strange stone chamber a calm bull stands.
An ink that can't exist writes the words *Deathhealth*
Upon a page that is & is not immortal.
The words are written as a single word.
The bull has hunger, & magic patience.
In each of my fists I have a lone kernel
Of grain from the basket in the alcove.
If I am snakelight, I can shine inside;
If I lose my composure & gain my soul,
There will be proof of how earthy I am.
My palms grow moist to hand me miracles,
Rain, bliss: with open mind & tight-closed fists,
I am not sure just what this gesture is
Except a gripping way to celebrate
Existence's stints as viscera, the jewel
That's wild perishability & verse
Set in—Someday I'll have a little girl!—
A daimon diadem of condensations
Flung far, feral, *lives*, gilded & retooled
For all, for all the timeless ritual:

I give its mouth my hand, hands, opening
To shock, possessed, each, of a tiny plant,
                    Sufficiency.

VII.

Daybreak after nine nights beyond the pale
In deepest vivisepultural earth.
I do look fetching in my shawl & veil

Of crowning dates & trailing sprouts well worth
The work of their gestation; I took pains,
& I am glad.   It's time now to give birth

To my freedom, & to that of my friends.
—*Not everyone locates* THE ANIMAL!
Someone is shouting from where darkness ends.

—*She's coming out bringing the snakes & bull!*
—*What if she wears the self-made greenery?*
—*She must be told it's all not possible.*

The oblong stone was partly moved away
From the great hole. I stand with my dear Bo*void*
& viper friends & see the light of day.

—*The bull must stay behind!* Now it's annoyed!
Do help it out. —*Forget about those snakes!*
It's only two who wish to be employed

In upper Greece; the rest cannot forsake
Their duties here. —*We won't help you one bit!*
I mount Bo*void* & the earth begins to shake,

The giant rock falling inside the pit,
Breaking into a sort of ramp affair
We climb. A rockslide that's commensurate

With our need for a hefty, earthly stair
Creates itself under each persuasive hoof:
We're out! The shawl flies off somewhere.

The snakes choose to land on some old temple's stoop.
I close my eyes, my head drops to the side;
I savor the death of which I'm living proof:

The prayer, Art, parure of the inside
Of deepest everything, can flaunt demise
Live in the amber of its formal pride!

* * *

Completing my five-act initiation poem was my lovingly
prepared meal & conversation . . .

(I served raw beef in peaches of great size
& succulence. My cook replaced each pit
With well-dressed meat. Each peach was a disguise

Of its unaltered self, with snakes on it,
Sweet twists of dates & nutmeats.) Art's equal feast
Shares freedom honorably distributed

Into the sacrifice that's form reprised
As the initiatives, births, deaths, beyond
How art serves . . . you!
                    I was at this point seized

By sated guests, & choked screaming a wound
Into my art. What can survive as space within
A love scene's lack of depth?   Two Dooms respond,

Old Fury types, when I ask what has gone on.
—It does appear you're fructifying death.
—A world cracked into sexes, was that fun ?

There isn't much good news. They sigh one breath,
—There couldn't be. Still, it's *a* Mystery.
—I bet the moon gives you a girl! Child? Yes!

I can't die now! But my self, voice, hope, leave me.
—See, hear, taste, grieve behind your painted mask
In silence. — Rest, then think *how to get free.*

How is the animal? I think to ask.
It's drinking rain collected in a tub
And fattening itself on tenderest grass.

VIII.

My Life in Art

I soaked the thresholds porous with my love
Of art; I'm the initiated dead:
    (Spelunking's what they murder to reprove,

      So each night for these five hundred years I've wept
      Initiate words to help me to endure
      A living death in this framed oubliette

      I know as a romance's craquelure.
      I executed ecstasy myself;
      Now I am killed into a love affair

      All by myself. I'm empty in the wealth
      Of color I gave flaking Giulio's
      Retainers, & I'm empty in the vale

      Of painted flowers, emptiest in those
      Because the earthiest reality
      Which finds a way to show its face means most—

      Each shows a blooming painted face!—to me.
      I executed everything concerned
      Artistically, but concerned Italy

      Clapped me inside a place no one's yet learned
      How to escape, the fretwork of womanly poise
      We have designed because our bodies burn

      For love, & sometimes baby girls or boys,
      & often for the gnosis manifest
      In art, & always for the worth a man enjoys.

What if Love entered here to, now, request
My nakedness, shatter my frame with need?
I'd look his way, & smile, & drop the dress,

This scab of pigment, art, in which I bleed
Poor love to nothingness? Initiate
Experience dies in lust's mouth of dust & lead;

Old union's pentimento like a slit
That's almost access, grace, marks my body's grief
Love's shade's too buried to be conduit

To my release, & recedes, a lost motif.
My work, *Initiation: The Deep Frieze,*
One nonagon, joins, in comic relief,

Death, Women, Trance, Food, Immortalities,
Art, Babies, Bulls & Snakes. But I was killed
Not into that but died in the debris

Of flop adultery I'd one day spilled
Upon a canvas to articulate
How much passion needs art. My killers filled

My exposé with me. I can't create
A cult of independence from within
The confines of an icon in a crate

Shipped out of Italy into the din
Of history I hear & feel; I taste
The death outside this painting like a skin.

A world, each world, is slowly laid to waste,
But in every age someone approaches me,
Sees through the scene, & claims to see my face.

I'm crated & uncrated, auctioned, hung, rehung, taken down,
blanketed, shipped, shipped. I endure a provenance that takes
me from Italy through Switzerland to France & eventually to
twentieth-century Britain:

How odd I'm not a simple murderee;
I did not die, though death is everywhere
The human art, even in Bloomsbury:

I did hang over someone with soft hair,
& many books, a well-considered opinion
Life's worth something as art. I was moved by her:

So moved, I am restored! Through her I'm given
The means to leave this flat *succès d'estime:*
We think back through our pigments if we're women

Who are works of art: I *think* this is the time
The thought of pigment so implies the brush
I chose, I *feel* the brush and start to climb

My cerebration of its bristles' plush;
I think, I climb: I think it is enough
To think the long-gone handle is a crutch,

A prop that now implies my touch,
The heat of creativity I get
From my life in art, *my life;* it's very much

Me, I think, to travel thoughtfully & let
Whatever I can think of have its way
With me: it's my way out & delicate

As murder in reverse, what I won't think of!)
I think . . . I am . . . aroused by mastery today!
I'll soak this threshold porous with my . . . art.

IX. Studio Work

The five-hundred-and-twenty-six-year-old soul of me pours out of the painting called The Joust *and manifests itself bodily in the art studio and home of a London painter who must go nameless. I appear to be a charming and talented young artist with no real knowledge of antiquity, my antiquity. The lover is also talented. But in a few months' time, I, pregnant, thoughtful, roll over in a bed perched above a packed valise and am moved to say:*

> I dreamed I robbed a bank with you, your form
> In front of me, crumpling: I held your hand
> Over my heart, its beating held you to me.
>
> I didn't have a gun stuck to your head;
> I didn't have a gun. Your hostage love
> Was my best shot: I will not break this man
>
> If these kind, moneyed bank clerks will just give
> Me funds enough to leave him, and the time
> In that drab vestibule to overask,
>
> Well, am I good? Your kind of good? Real good?
> The day I stepped into my canvases,
> (You never step into your canvases.)
>
> I made a kind of matter of the holes,
> Our art's equivalent of what you felt
> When my sexed hand pressed yours to my sexed need:
>
> I need to rob a bank with you, you dick!
> The take's the Sacred Mysteries, my death,
> A fear-created tenure in the vault
>
> We've known as an old oil misnamed *The Sport,*
> *Una certa illustrazione*
> Life in this flat with you's familiar

As dust: I'd rather initiatedness.
You'd stare me down each time you visited,
Sniff at my grime, then turn, turn back, then go.

There is something ekphrastic, Love, that you—
And how you love *The Sport!*— do not yet know:
The *Orpheus* is to be had with food . . .

So pull the sheet over yourself to your chin.
Let just your head stick out, floating on the bed.
I'll eat a peach & leave you all choked up.

—Your secret paintings are not nice, but good.
The portrait of your lover is not nice,
But good. The holes you make with feet are too

Predictable. You compensate for this
Predictability with your raw nerve.
This isn't bad. I don't do this myself,

But it's not bad. The picture of the girl
With her bare foot thrust through nine canvases
Is masterful in execution, and . . .

And what?—*Your light on her taut, rosy arch*
Evokes in me a sexual response.
Foolish, since you don't love me anymore.

I fear you never did.
                      This is my dream.
The studio has come apart in time.
I'm not beneath a master like a sheet.

Prestidigitation, 1856

A beadle strokes a ruffle stiff. *Worsted*
  Like an itching powder coats him, suits him.
His shoes are Mary Janes, *and snagged wool socks*
  Torture her *corns. He's* . . . No! She's Poetry.

Look there! A governess, Psychology,
  In sensible attire, insensible.
The upstairs maid made love to her tonight.
  Jane isn't quite herself; profundity

Is incompletely hers: vaginal pang
  Traps Jane's pleasure, binds what's left of release
In mid-orgasmic tourniquets made of
  The meta-hysterical. Ring for that maid!

Marie is History, and she does come.
  Jane will not have Religion's child and leave
The manor in disgrace. She loves Marie!
  Dear Poetry just taxes everyone.

United Artists

Oh my god it is Mary Pickford alive, her skin
like quicksand with Pan-Cake and rouge un-
able to effect a subterfuge at all; she's edited
dirt—Shit!—I drive a Continental to to
reconnive a break-down through her conti-
nuity, huge kaleidoscopic rough-assemblage
I gouge in one flash cut; a zillion scenes ar-
rive and I am caught in all of them and thrive
aghast. I'm but a filmy past seen through. I'm
in the big house now, the big chair, *you*, like
we are really something we deprive each other
of when we are separate; I screen you on my
face. You say, "Say what?"

Le Réalisme Fantastique
de Berthe Bovary Lipschitz en Anglais Américain

What can I say? I know the textile trade,
Its crafts, its business, inside and out.
Each side of the Atlantic is the same;
The goods are compromised; the compromise
Is good for business, and this is good
For one short run of what's past beautiful:
Her fringe, his faille, your piece-good peonies.
The purchase of the short run is what's style.

I am that thing's insupportable child.
Do you remember me? The Bovary,
The one, who has survived adultery
As art? The babe? The faint-producing girl?
The one farmed out to nurse in that poor house
With Fame, a perfume ad, hung on shoe nails?
A complicated, simple entity,
A mad cap clutched tight by *Charbovari*.

The gossips ask so much: *Why didn't she*
Transform his love, his masculinity,
Into the thing she craved? It would have been
Like pulling teeth, but still she should have pushed.
If men weren't hard, who would be interested?
I pushed my father once and he was dead,
A mass beneath the arbor and its shade;
The constancy I knew before the mills.

I landed at my grandmother's; she died.
An aunt, all kinds of poor, then took me in.
I worked at cotton mills for years for change.
The glyphs on my grown hands match my scarred cheek;
My mother'd elbowed me one afternoon
Right past a chest, into a curtain hook.
I have a well-healed gash. One rain-stained day
I walked it, musing, past a nearby farm:

One sow, couch-vast, lay suckling in her mess
Her many little infants, then a man—
I should have seen him shadow me?—began
A litany of wild remarks. He'd hide
Behind the barn, a tree, the pigs. He'd scream
My name with expletives, his mouth the maw
Of my worst fears: *You* are *your mother's girl!*
The sow stirred in her sleep; one nurseling died.

The man—a tramp—picked up the fresh-dead pig.
Its mouth was open; white milk dribbled out.
I stood too still. *My tit, my pretty tit,*
He cried, then opened up his shirt and feigned
It was a breast, the corpse. He preened. I froze.
He grabbed its haunches with both hands and thrust
The thing between his legs, jerked up its snout.
You can't come to the mother save through me.

He ran at me. The rain had made an ocean
In heaped manure, and I fell in to garner
Detritus as tiara; slops as earrings;
One mud-glove pair; one waterbeetle necklace;
One sin-diluvial chemise, all whetted
To revelations: belly, bush and nipples;
One divot boot; one mule of pondscum, worm-trimmed;
And last, the pork corsage he piled on, fleeing.

The saturation taught my sex its sex;
A gaggle warped this wisdom with goose noise.
I thought of sitting up, of dry, dry hair.
I mused a crematorium's hot air,
A rising song, inventing heat, its lift . . .
I scaled—though I was lying, yes—my mold.
I nearly was out of my mind: a voice:
Are you fallen? Or have you met foul play?

A man; a gloveless hand; a horse; a ride
Across the sun-abandoned countryside
In man-warm clothes; our hat; our flask
Of torrid brandy's porous heat; our task
Of conversation left to road with hoof,
Until, *Live here, beneath my father's roof.*
My mother's dead, but you may have her shoes,
If you'll accept our aid;—our door:—we're Jews.

They don't speak proper French, Alsatian Jews.
They're German-like, Maurice, Michel and Paul.
(New names.) They've started a new factory.
They brought three hundred people from Alsace.
They left their clothworks there for full-fledged France.
They love the France that thinks them Prussian spies.
They've clothed, employed and educated me;
And once the warm Michel discussed his God:

We don't know what It is, but we're Its Jews.
It's clear, in time, It wants; It's needed us,
Our held-up history, our gravity,
For Its sole moon, for the fidelity
Of matter to its tether. Marry me.
I want you faithless, Catholic or Jew.
But why? *The sight of you soaked through was sex like It.*
Forgive the likeness, God, mine to a Jew!

The next day at the factory I saw
The man, Maurice, my father-, soon,-in-law,
Caress and strike his younger son, Michel.
He kicked his precious offspring in the crotch.
Two women brought eight women to the men:
Potential brides, Jewish, much-parented,
Quite unlike me. A rabbi touched my cheek;
And swans kept swimming on their polished stuffs.

I wouldn't choose this thing if I could choose,
My father figure said to me that night.
It is like choosing to be God himself.
We'll famine friendship with the world at large.
We'll drought their hopes of insufficiency,
The mass gentility, surviving them
All, insufficiently. (We'll *Sinai* fêtes
However irreligious we become.)

At dawn I wrote a poem in my room.
I call it *Ruth.* I wrote it for the truth,
The lost Naomi I will trail to death
In handmade shoes, though I'm departed now
With men on board a ship bound for New York.
—*We could improve on Lipschitz, couldn't we?*
—*I'm looking into Lincoln presently.*
And now it is my wedding night below:

I'm so afraid, Michel. *Of love?* Of death
By love. What is the Jewish afterlife?
It's stones on top of tombstones, yours and mine, . . .
Stones? . . . *left there by the children we create.*
Just kiss me now, and sleep here by my side.
Perhaps my child would bring a figurine
Of jade, pink jade . . . *I think not, dear.* Perhaps
A line of verse etched on the tomb? *Good night.*
Perhaps a line I write myself? Michel?

You want to know what I will make of love.
You thrill to learn that I am beautiful,
And scared. *You'*d kill to know if I am good:
If I will meet a man in rented rooms;
If I will make my corset's lacing hiss,
A snake in genesis, undoing it;
Will I take arsenic as payment due
My sex's interest? What do I dream?

I dream my mother loves me for myself.
I dream, in fact, I am myself her dream.
She's holding me. There are no bodices,
No suicidal promises of loves
Like fairy tales. Her hands on me, my fat,
My soul-implying thighs, are hands, not alms
To give poor noblemen in nightmare dreams.
She touches me. We dream ungrasping touch.

I cry new tears onto her cuticles.
Her pretty and unbeautiful dry hands
Create a manger for my bowed black head
Because I manger them in my own grip.
I cradle cradling: Each fingertip,
A baby, will be nursed—I'll nurse—to health
With each wept kiss; and if I can, I'll sing
That if there's sweet romance, we are that thing.

But I awake to see America.
I re-receive a vision smart in black:
A sex whose sole redress is sex, whose whole
Unmastered book of days is charity,
When it is not the most pathetic cant,
Volition as the courage to attract
And to be acted on.
                          Volition-verse,
I'll dream my mother's kiss, and wake to you.

I'll take my stirring husband in my arms—
I'll be quite Jewish doing it—and love
The way I write: I'll love the way I write.
Dear Father faith, Dear Mother dream, Dear Child,
Dear Mate who's sensible, and warm, and hot,
Dear Nation whose vast compass is your plot,
(You province of new bourgeois demi-gods!)
I'll be some kind of realist, and write.

for my Alison Blythe

Lazorra the Vixen

. . . like an oblique and illicit blade . . .
—Roland Barthes

In seedy shacks, quick with the chickens and the chicks,
I always know which ones have asked their deaths of me.

The kill remains the practical turnstile this world proffers;
I palpate chick dissatisfaction, open-mouthed.

Awejaw!   Featherbloodteeth!   Pawclawawe!
                                                My kits greet me
After we've polished off demolishings once hens.

Next day I pass a house, a plump cock in my mouth,
And smell like death a woman's total loss of nerve.

She's martyring a puling baby into fear
Of union and its loss. The husband's just stepped out.

I don't leave her a kill, but return as my kits doze
To drop one fox-gnawed beak on her old welcome mat.

She's crying numbers now, and crying something fierce.
A sister, separated, clucks, "Our laws lack teeth."

What Happy Women Feel*

I now pull down, from off my collarbones,
A magic fringe of spiritskin, a growth
Which has an anchoring, blood-ruching, at my waist,
And a beginning—stitches!—in my sex.

The physic of the soundless popping feeling
Filling me open as I tug and free
Thirty-six hundred invisible strings,
Is brutal self-correction given the sack.

How will the nipples, breastbone, heart, lungs, breath
Sustain the release of the dense flesh web,
Each thread a day of my life lived away
From sense, a harp-y vest strung to glut with woe?

The pattern of my will, its action in
Unsparing agitation, inquiry,
Is, too,—how?—humanely, a needle in my sleep,
Soulflesh exposed in amulet tatters.

I pull a strip: I never have had what
Are called relations with a human soul.
It cannot be lovemaking I have had.
What lover worth the name would simply leave

The veil intact, having kissed another
Yarn in place, hallowing another day
Of error hiding, making known, remove!
Remove the wear of endless, loveless days:

I'm self-erected, -entered, -decorated:
A dandelion's shaken path through space;
The tentacles of inessential time;
A hairshirt skirt of years thinned out by fear

And threaded through propriety by chance.
I mean that I was born American
And vulviform: I am but literate,
Yet, dear, aroused in spite of everything.

A succubus shall kiss me in a cloud
Of the fabric of my freedom, and time,
For all time, must hang around us like a shroud,
And I do suffer this virginity

As old souls enter fetuses, finally.

* *a phrase from a letter by Edith Wharton to Morton Fullerton*

Doyenne du Comice

Do not misunderstand my short career
As kitchen help. The man of the house can't see
What's dirty and to do when he sees me,
Consumption, on a dish with other pears.

Pears rears, a ring, announce Pear Charlotte's there,
Just past the filthy old rotisserie,
Pear William spilled along a recipe-
backed poem, on a bill for Charlotte, Pear.

The *Poires Hélène*, chilling, have room to spare
In the refrigerated space set free
Of food save pears, pear by-products, pear trees
Of marzipan and marzipan dove pairs.

The mistress of the house has gone upstairs.
She's with my sister and her *poésie*
Not long; she comes for me redundantly.
It's why they call my substance flesh; skin, skin.

The Draw

For who shall change with prayers or thanksgivings
The mystery of the cruelty of things?
                    —Algernon Charles Swinburne

I draw you into my arms, and the sheets
Go warm red, acid, muscle-undulant,
Cradling us in some kind of whipped-up sea

Of jaundice-and-blush; the sheets are having the sex
That's like every bitter fraudulence I
Baby into poetry like being.

We cannot speak the sex that's having us
Because its violences are our parents'.
Injury, a boy, premisunderstands

He is my father and is infamy
In sheets we think we are before we know
We're their agitation, their excuse,

Their opportunity to draw us in
To the saturation of a moving fiction:
We are in bed; the bed is not in us.

A classical figure has vomited
Her own drapery and it proceeds
To argue with its orgins and to drop

The argument when I forget to love
The fact I was invented of their pain,
And I may be invented once again.

Woo

*The awareness of the fact that the pleasure of killing is
the truth, charged with horror, for one who does not
kill, can remain neither obscure nor tranquil, and it
forces life into an unlikely frozen world, where it tears
itself apart.*

—Georges Bataille

What's it to AIDS
If everyone's,
Initiate's
To lay person's,
Best pleasure *is*
Proximity
To homicide?

Is protest then,
In part, delay
That breeds contempt,
Impatience, rage,
Unconscious lust
For some kind of
Proximity
To homicide?

Who's Woo? What's Woo's
Shock cinema
Of Hong Kong crime
To AIDS? Some cure
For that contempt,
The killing truth?
His cuts may be
A place to freeze,
Parallel to health.

On the Extensive, Publisher-Executed Bowdlerization of Ray Bradbury's *Fahrenheit 451*

Just because you're paranoid
Doesn't mean they're not
Out to gut you.

for Brenda and George Carlin

Tellurion

—*Why do you use such words!* She scolded me,
Speak simply, cleanly. (She was plainly irked.)
—Tellurion.
        —*Like that, Tolurmeon!!?#!!?!*

                 *   *   *   *   *

Tellurion defines itself for me
As a tub of flesh built of my grammar school kisses
Practiced into pillows, rehearsed on my wrists,
Perfected on two fingers of my right hand
Made to flex open, substitute for lips.
Dear living bath, hot tub of vivid skin,
Do you suffer? You're not like porcelain
And are, dear thing, possessed *of* religion
And *by* the miracle of your strange life-
And-fate as the one flesh tub on earth, born, kissed
Into warm existence by fantasy
Eroticized, kissed at daily, and fed
The little passion-sessions of bright, dark
Adolescents your ball-&-claw feet thrill!
I ache to put my lover's tears in you,
Add every masturbation's spit and spills
To you, add rain, all buds' damp trims, add me.
What fresh Bonnard will capture me in your hold
Of sperm, dew, spigoted lubricity?
(You insinuate perspicacity
Is just art-fed corporeality.)
I steal the things a poet needs, of course:
I help myself; it helps to lift things from
The world of scientific instruments.
        I get so sentimental about terms
        I've redefined. The English call this wet.
            Let's don't resist redefinitions: thrills:
                You'll only know my season by these depths.

A *Marschallin* (Your Choice) Sightseeing Craterside at Volcanoes National Park Is Addressed by What Appears to Be a Twenty-eight-year-old Man in a Dress

I see you're very near the edge, Bichette.
I'll come too close and set our skirts ablaze
If I'm not careful. And I'm not careful yet
Though I've had more than ten years to appraise
Carelessness, and care. I've trailed you now for days,
Put on, stripped off, this rag and pantaloons.
It's not first dawn, but might I serve, your grace?
We have, and they'll be timeless, afternoons.

You know my life: a rose, a marriage bed;
The morning sickness; stillbirth; births; the face
Of what I'd seen in tears, in silhouette–
Quite inexpert episiotomies;
A healthy son, then two, the commonplace
Epiphanies, awe; all . . . I won't impugn.
Your Breakfast's Tea, and hot despite delays.
Let's have it . . . : 'Twill be timeless afternoon.

The light is harsh here, platinum, dead red.
The world's making its bed from bleak forays
In rock. Once, one dawn, fine silk georgette
And poetry were tossed off . . . as embrace
To me, as features of embrace, as if taste,
Haute comedy intact, shall, good, festoon
All loves. A love may work, but it rarely plays.
We have. There still is time this afternoon . . . .

ENVOY
Just look: my hot, wet *eau de Nil broché* 's . . .
But heat here's mouth's suttee: lips, flames, maroon
My hope of . . . taste . . . in all your smile betrays
You have *today, tomorrow* . . .
                              'Afternoon.

In Memoriam James Merrill

39

Coole Jerk

When we were all the nine-and-fifty swans,
When all our multiplicities took flight
Through just one other's vast encouragement,
Pleasure was not a dream one could wake from.

Why are we fifty-nine wild swans? you sang,
For fifty-nine's an odd number, of course.
All that we are, I crooned, is in this mass,
And one part of us has not wed for life:

I don't believe in you for me; I don't
Believe you're not that mournful thing, a man
Who dreams and wakes hell-bent on capturing
Song's ecstasy in images of song.

Who, lover by lover, is still clamorous,
Is some white sovereignty that oversees?

Of *Dicebas quondam solum te nosse* . . .

I'm Gaius, when I'm your preference. By Jove,
We crawl through some strange world where gods aren't dead
But live to partner you in squalid love.

I'm Gaius now, recalling what you said:
The sex is good or bad, but not the same
With . . . Them? I cannot seem disinterested.

A father loves the child who bears his name
A fraction of the way that I love you,
You trash. And then there's mother-love to blame.

Being Gaius is what I am called to
When, Lesbia, you call your lovers off:
I know you now, the dirt: you're scum clean through:

This makes me crave you, hole. *How's that?* you laugh.

Bumptious Unction

I. Lusting, after Berryman

I quest a fantasy, I'll tell it you.
Today's a Sunday. Let's meet Monday, eh?
By then I know you will have written a
Sonnet for me, to best your rest. Say, do
Have it by heart. (Of course in pocket too.)
The sun will out. Sweet, meet me rising, lay
Me on our made hay here, faith's bier, our place,
And hard kiss me, my Boiler-Maker. Woo
Me true as you can, well, conceive. Undo
My blouse. (I'll be beneath.) Then eye breasts, say,
You want the sonnet now? (I'll not say nay.)
Proceed with feeling; press your pants' suit through
To me; relieve our clothes; stay poised and quote
Your op'ning line . . . and then give all you wrote.

II. Recreation

The jeans; the Buddy Holly eyeglass frames;
The pert gold curls behind the ears; the same
Stuff straighter, razor-cut across the game-
obsessed boy's brain; the father-shared three names;
The Converse lows; the tear-hot eyelash flames
Around the eyes as blue as *À Madame;*
The wart close to the thumb; the wart that came
After the first was burnt; the tongue; the shames

Of passes thrown to not-our-team five times
In one sad half; the soft, self-quilting kiss—
As pluralist, as singular, as sex—
Before and during sex; the sex; the climbs
In jeans and All-Star sneaks through screens like this
Fine mesh, a life, a list: the gasp, the kicks.

III. The Lover of the Queen of the Fortunate Islands

Upon arriving at the court, you fall
Into the depths of a voluptuous sleep.
Your form, the forms of others, line the hall,
A mass of perfect gentlemen, each deep
In his requisite dream. When you awake,
The subject of your dream is written on
Your forehead plain as day. You're scared; you ache
To read yourself. So many men are gone.
Ones stamped *Dominion Over All* were shown
The door and war. A score of other men
Depart as mateless, heat-mad minks. Who's thrown
Back to his mother's arms?
                                        You dreamed the Queen
In all her mystery and need. A phrase
And fate mark you: *Compassion's all that stays.*

John Fowler
Thinking of Pinking
Pure Silk Taffeta Triangles
On Behalf of Pauline de Rothschild

In an Albany apartment, or set as it is rather idiosyn-
cratically known, Fowler found himself working for a
client with very individual ideas about lifestyle.
      —Chester Jones, *Colefax & Fowler,*
      The Best in English Interior Decoration

To the Trade

It stiffens always French, your Anglaisness,
She'd laughed. *I just must say "Marie Antoinette!"*
The decorator's need is to suggest . . . ,
She'd winked. Suggestive or suggestible.
What you don't know of curtains can't be known.
And "Curtains!" is American for doom.
Silk is, you are, all I'll have of death, Monsieur.

Can Englishness stiffen American?
Should she have said Frenchly? Frenchily? Stiffens?
It always stiffens Frenchly, Englishness?
Did I not take her meaning properly?
Hers was improper usage, wasn't it?
And not a compliment. No, not a bit.
French is made difficult by Englishness?

A dog worries a bone to good effect.
My way with worry's all repulsiveness.
It's some repellent quality of mine
That comes out in a Francophiliac
Spasm. I don't care what you meant, *Madame.*
I'm awed that you said syllables to me
In our two languages; no, in our three.

Whatever *things* we said were *Albanese.*
Lord Byron lived here; now our poetries:
For throw rugs, pelts, whelps of a warm, nude floor;
The spaciousness let be; the walls made putty;
A window's oyster baste of taffeta . . . .
I'd kill to be there now, your Albany,
Our work undone, *Madame,* our work undone.

I'm not at odds with what I have become.
I don't use tradesman's entrances nowadays,
Not Lady Colefax's, not anyone's;
Don't eat alone in Petworth's nursery.
I'm not the thing "That Nancy" sent abroad.
Victoria: I board a night Pullman:
Voilà, Paris for breakfast: *pain, et mon coeur.*

Let's muse you triangles for . . . valances,
Sheer hundreds, pinked, so no unraveling.
I dream my man cuts out the draperies;
One pattern pair in cotton, two in silk:
He hesitates once with his pinking shears;
The fall is harmed! Fresh goods, and go again!
One cannot be faint-hearted with a blade.

Knowledge of you, such as I have, translates
Abjection *lit à la polonaise,* creating
Our spare design as violence we succeed:
Your bed is all alone in your rare space.
It's brutally singular, wit-canopied.
Its placement lets me hail hope perfectly,
My spirit hard upon pure reason, freed.

Four Days

After the birth of her daughter, she was bitterly disap-
pointed and "it was four days before I looked at the
child."

—Jürgen Kesting, *Maria Callas*

Birth's pangs' bleed wringings, concentricities,
two bodies' pooled interpolatedness
of heldness, which is everything, and squeeze,
a heldness unbecoming what it is.

I'll lose my voice, but not my sense of this;
The mother is impossible to please:
her son has died. *I'm* born. She won't caress
this insult a girl body is for days:

I crack dispersed—cells, cells fly dead—without touch,
leaking the skin's needs screaming like a heart
falling and flung open into ice down a dark
voice of pulse in *vernix* that won't hold: voice.

A voice can be a physical contact.
The intake breath now answers me in me
And I'm the narrative of those four days.
We live to kill the women that won't hold.

My Robe Is Open

My robe is open. And its ermine's live,
Three litters' worth, collapsed, nursed, napping: trim
For several acres' violet velvet cut
To full inadequacy: closureless,—
The frogs are frogs!— it means to redress clothes.
It, animality, lives to expose
My breasts, their roses, and my hedge of hair's
Roots' earthy furrow's cultivated spring.
The angel of the lord is whispering:
I've good news and bad news. She's turned out, too;
A mien and raiment I can see right through.
You have the perfect lover for me! *We*
Have, Majesty, the perfect love for you!

For me, The Giantess! Inside the gorge,
The hollow of my throat, a choker king
Hangs slack on links of sterling ministers
Dismissed—Unpolished!—from my treasured drawers.
Say, what's the really disappointing part—
I need a big kiss. Huge.— of your bad news?
Your love is, shall we say, a pregnancy.
But I am in my prime this afternoon!
The proper love for you has not been born.
It's clitoridectomy via neglect.
You have to wait. NO WAY. *You will conceive . . .*
Of love . . . My age! *. . . in fresh . . .* His youth! *. . . new ways . . .*
I plan to behave badly. *We thought so.*

I spit a pond; the frogs immerse themselves,
Then labor, croaking, up my piping's silk
And sit down hard.—*The child's* your *child*!—They puff.
One ermine chews my hair to some new do.
My velvet's now a crush. . . . *She will not hear.*
Well, I'll disport myself; it's all the rage:
Each "gem" is a marquise, and horrible.
I grab my toothpick, Mr. President.
Slave-bracelets, despot-earrings, anklet-popes
Should be, are, put away in my strong box
With piles of bright aristocratic studs
I can no longer use; I've lost my shirt!
My robe's open . . . I am waiting . . . to hurt.

Pretext

I. The Real Dream

I walked the streets of Paris, France.
The time was two or three A.M., I think.
I met one Hippolyte Castille. We talked.
He had something to do. I went with him.
He felt obliged to give his latest book
To Madam Something at some whorehouse place.
This book of Hippolyte's was judged obscene;
Obscenity could grease our way within.
Obscenity, virility: who knows.
We'd never dared a thing without a book.

Well, once inside I was uncomfortable.
I sensed, I *knew*, my penis was exposed.
My trousers were unbuttoned and agape.
It was indecent to present myself
In such a way even in such a place.
I noticed that my feet were wet and bare.
I'd waded through a puddle by the stairs
And hadn't noticed till I noticed it.
I had to wash my feet. I vowed to wash
My feet two times. One time before the sex.
And once again before I left the house.

I did go up the stairs. From that time on,
I did not think about the book at all.
I do not know what happened to the book.
I saw large galleries, all badly lit
Like old cafes, old reading rooms, the like.
The prostitutes were talking to the men.
Some men were very young, were, in fact, boys.
I felt intimidated. I was sad.
I was afraid someone would see my feet.
I did look down; somehow I had one shoe.
And later on, I had two shoes somehow.

The walls had sketches; not all were obscene.
I did see architecture, didn't I?
And some Egyptian figures in cheap frames.
I gave myself to this bordello's art
As one might give oneself to one's dear one.
I could not dare approach the prostitutes.
A group of pictures: birds: mad hues, gore's hues!
And eyes that were alive! I'll swear to that.
And many birds were incompletely formed.
Each picture had a note: this whore, that whore,
Aged what, gave birth to this, that, fetal thing
On such and such a date in such a year.

It did occur to me that art like this
Was not conducive to romantic thoughts.
The funds for this museum and whorehouse
Had been provided by the publishers
Of *Le Siècle*, the world's worst newspaper.
How forward to link medicine and sex!
Their mania for science, for the spread
Of knowledge, for progressiveness, breeds death.
I don't know how I know financial things.

Just then I saw the pedestal, its *self*,
A monstrous thing born in this very house.
Its face was pleasing, Orientalish,
All tan but pink-and-green around some parts.
A large black object, something like a snake
Was wound around its body and its limbs.
This object came from deep within its head,
And was elastic but heavy and long.
The head could not support the object's weight.
The body must support the mass of coils.

The monster took his supper with the girls
And hated this. He told me so at length.
He had to struggle to the supper room
And then arrange his coils so he could dine.
This all was burdensome. There was no help.
He barely maintained access to his mouth,
The kind of access one requires to eat.
He talked all right. He fascinated me.
I stopped myself from touching his strange flesh.

* * *

And then "my woman" moved the furniture.
"My woman" moved some things, real things, around.
I then transcribed the dream she broke in me.

II. Cock Provenance

You harbor my transcription of my dream
Of Baudelaire's old dream inside the sleep you are
Because I kissed it into you. I pushed too far.
I kissed you much too Frenchily. Pity.
And now I've come back crying for my kiss.
I'm every wretched theft sex payment is.
I'm in your bedroom, crying for my kiss.
You don't wake up. I'm crying for my kiss.
You won't wake up. I know. I speak up for what's mine:

You do not need the monster or the art,
The so cold feet, the sadness, the new book, for friends.
I'm fealty ... but ... where childhood's vise ... is voice ...
   vice extends.
I hover broken over you; lips part.
I don't molest the bodies close to you.
I can't explain myself although I do:
I thought you too were wet and lacked a shoe.
You're not a monstrous self's self-curlicue;
I am my own black mass, its birth's establishment.

I'm the plaything of dead dreamed sexfear.
You never really let it dandle your largesse.
Give back my furtle's pilfering gross nimbleness;
I need my stolen nightmare to finger!
I kiss you hard! Cough up the poet's pants!
I walk the streets of Paris, France.
The time is two or three A.M., ...

                              ... Bonne chance
To us: two futures, childhoods, dreamed against,
Slept with, one's trousers now unbuttoned and agape ...

                              for Patrick Brossard

He Is Our Greatest Poet of Blood

and I force him, his form, hulking, opaque, dense, deaf and impossible, to appear in a calm, infernal room of Rue's House this Los Angeles midnight. He's quite dead in his own wild Spanish way and, too, perambulating, porous with all he knows of composition and decomposing, a magical spectre, macabre, serene, a spherical bulk of body topped with his famous, crude, globular skull, his hands grabbing through the frayed braidwork of a fancy blanket, raiment, his material and the night an amalgam of the fresh pressures of shadows, sediment making the air here particular, thick.

I am every hysteria. The women and children with AIDS sleep fitfully in the little rooms of Rue's House, and somehow I have fabricated, produced, two colossal lenses, glass circles that I know derive from the windshield and rear window I've torn from my own car outside, torn and formed, ground into vision aids, with the bare hands of this dream of anguish. Old and unreal artist's materials fall from his wrap; I see them fall but I don't hear them land. Like him, I've found the world deafening. I represent all this as prose poetry.

In the crib there is one little rump up, the poor shape of a dying nine-month-old snuggled in a colorless suit of stretch terry, an extra layer of goose bumps. I have the dream of a skewer, several knives, the level head of a straight razor. The artist will not turn to me. Shall I offer to let the baby's life out between the two huge lenses, a petal saved between pages, the gist of a sandwich, the substance of a well-supported argument?

But the painter's face I find is something dark that stops, to my eyes, the hospice's, my, interior darkness. I guess the face: gristle, grisaille, flicks, drips, floating grease, insinuations of featureless strokes, the pointlessness of lines I cannot make out because they seem to enunciate the residues of numberless planes, a depths of originating dusts in a lithe, quell-less narrative. Is he a somnambulism, the great artist, the picture of silence?

Not silenced though silence-hearing, I can't control my pitch: YOU MUST PAINT THE WAR WITHIN THE BLOOD! I stumble on a metal folding chair; I'll hold it, hurl it, hit him square across the kidneys. I'll ram one of the rubber-tipped legs along his powdery old shin. He will hear me as pain. He's just an unwholesome, Spanish-speaking guy caught in a women's residence in the dead of a California night. This is Los Angeles: I know I can threaten him with authority. His wrap's got pouches with sketches he produces; it's Los Angeles: I laugh at his papers.

I can no longer know what laughter sounds like. A woman appears to be snoring near the place where I stand. She cannot prevent me from screeching a pitch, screaming a light into and through the lenses which I have hauled into this house and propped up on her bed without her consent. There is something sanguine between the circles, and I don't know if it is the baby's. Is it a palette's spawn? A flood of my own hysteria? Did I obtain it and glass it in? I know I am willing a monstrous, necessary tightening of the lenses, turning them without aid in opposite directions, finding a vision; I feel assured I am sacrificing my own heart's musculature to garner my one bio-ekphrastic twist of sorcery: ¡TIENES QUE PINTAR LA GUERRA DENTRO DE LA SANGRE!

He slowly roams the few rooms, and then raises the geometries of his hands along one small interior wall. He is not any less dust for this one bit of industry. He's undertaking the application of the kind of fragrant plaster that is not at all real, smells food-like more than architectural, smooths the wall's surface and is a cause of intolerable physical ecstasy in me; he moves separate from any sacrifice.

The artist turns his back on the women and children to cloud the wall with marks that are an accretion of disease given apperception, given theatre. I feared he'd try to render only the suffering human figures, that I would be magnetized by their displayed pain and while I could not help but worship them, while I kneeled, he'd escape forever, abandoning the burden of Rue's House. Can one pay with the whole heart for only art?

His dust, however, leaves a picture of a cellular, only an infinitely spiritual, anatomy; he hasn't given the disease a human face, and his is not an ethical creation, lacking a reductive view of a syndrome's tyranny, boasting, rather, black, blacker, complications: what seems to splint mere harm is shown to be the coagulated edge of supreme idiot violence fronting annihilation with what even cell-sized dismemberment does make to cohere:

The little girls are waking first; they call their mothers now.
Soon everyone in Rue's House dons a clean white cotton gown,

And we surmise their music from the movements of their mouths
And shy, haphazard dance steps breaking, brave, into unknown

Enactments, panic, parodies of panic, death satire
Danced violently by frightened little girls. A girl falls down.

The other girls fall down. The mothers slowly find the floor.
They do not like this game. One rises and gropes for the crib;

The baby is alive and kicks; her mother dances her
Up to the painting, presses her small back at it, holds, smears,

Then places her white-swaddled tummy's curve against it too.
She's printed all around now with *The War Within the Blood*.

Soon everyone is printed with *The War Within the Blood*.
They're dancing at incomprehensibility and time,

Each gifted now with infinite discernment, painted on;
The greatness in the art has summoned everything they are

To their dark reckoning: they're each a bodymind of grace
And trance: *lived death's pure inquiry and so serenity* . . .

They're not invaded innocences, they're now scrutinies,
Initiations, lives with access, strength and fluency

Enough to stay unmartyred by this opportunity
To know the reaches of a world's originality.

Hear the Abyss which precedes and, shepherding, comes after
Whatever you misname abysmal in experience.

The crook of art may steal you back to the gentle shepherd
Who steels you for your time with the father-maker of the world

Who, heard, recedes, melts into matrices, not so singular
As He, but which are, and how, the real opportunities

You have which are not the world, the world in you, the world to
*   come:*
Art does imply the deep material love of the Abyss

And poetry can always conjure up what this lack is,
Place mystery inside you and between the worlds at war

Inside you, baffling every hope of calling peace a death.

for Gregory B. Seymann, M.D.

A Marcel Wave

And can it be—it must!—I am the character of all time,
    Maman?
You are certainly pajama'd greatness in your cozy bed,
    Sweet child.
And can it be—it is?—inevitable some magnitude of
    Your soul
Has gone merely praised, that's underestimated,
    By me
And you'd prefer it kissed more thoroughly, with ever greater love,
    Right now?
Is there in the dark with you, with any, every, future you,
    A cry
That mourns I am downstairs, and plenitude seems not to be
    At hand?
I lavish on you here, palms, knuckles, nails, the loveliest
    Rare smooch
Made to comprehend deeply you as you wrap yourself in sleep
    This night.
It will increase itself in baby kisses each time you wave
    Bye-bye
At any, every, touching parting; you do know you have
    My word.

Notes

The epigraph to this volume is from "The Steeplejack" by Marianne Moore.

"Plath": "The first kind of twig to be found in the besom (witch's broom) is of course the birch, the tree of birth and rebirth. Then there is the hazel, which is the tree of fire, fertility, poetry, divination and knowledge. Finally comes the yew, the tree of death and resurrection. Looking at these woods, the message is quite simple. Only through birth will there be life. From that life will come poetry, art and knowledge. Yet because of birth, there must be death, and with death, rebirth or resurrection."
—Doreen Valiente & Evan Jones,
Witchcraft, A Tradition Renewed

"Of All of Literature, Art, Philosophy, Politics & Cuisine Now or Ever": "An experience in Colombia increased Botero's fascination with the solid, compact human form. In 1955, after his return from Europe, he saw in Bogotá a performance by a Spanish troupe of dwarf *toreros*. One dwarf, mounted on two others who played the horse, attacked the bull: 'The disproportion increased the sense of danger,' Botero recalled. 'This lent the spectacle an extraordinary plasticity—the bodies, piled up on each other and welded into a block, appeared to me like a ghostly apparition of my own painting.'"
—Werner Spies, *Fernando Botero*

"The Imaginary Portraits of Simonetta Vespucci": The goodness and beauty of a historical Simonetta Vespucci are celebrated in *Stanze per la giostra* by Angelo Poliziano, completed in 1478. Simonetta was by marriage a kinswoman of Amerigo Vespucci from whose name *America* derives. She is depicted as the mistress of Giuliano de'Medici, the younger brother of Lorenzo, who was murdered in Florence Cathedral. Simonetta died while Poliziano was half-way through his poem praising her and transforms into *Fortuna* in his text; Giuliano's death caused the poet to abandon his *Stanze*. Poliziano's *Orfeo*, a proto-opera, is the *Orpheus* that begins my poem. There is scant evidence to support my poem's assertions that Simonetta Vespucci was an initiate of ancient mysteries, a painter, a homicide, or possessed of the mystical knowledge of how to survive love or death by becoming a work of art. Wait, this last is a bald-faced lie.

"Lazorra the Vixen": "Zorro—the fox so cunning and free / Zorro—make the sign of the Z!" So goes the theme song (by Norman Foster and George Burns) of the 1950s hit TV show *Zorro*. "Z is the letter of mutilation."–Roland Barthes, *S/Z*, translated by Richard Miller. The epigraph is also from *S/Z*.

"The Draw": The epigraph is from Swinburne's "Atalanta in Calydon."

"Woo": The epigraph is from *Inner Experience* by Georges Bataille, translated by Leslie Boldt. The poem considers the hospital sequence from *Hard Boiled*, 1992, directed by John Woo. Jason Jacobs (*Sight & Sound*, October '95) points out, "Woo uses every technique and every type of squib to deliver some of the most sustained and unlikely gunfire sequences on film. At the end of *Hard Boiled* the two cop heroes Chow Yun-Fat and Tony Leung are working their way through some hospital corridors, leaving a war-crime's worth of dead bad guys in their wake. Their squib-soaked progress is filmed and choreographed with a steadicam in one take: sometimes the sound and action groan into slow-motion (usually to extend a wounding frenzy), then groan back up to normal speed; the two even get into a lift and start cleaning out the *next* floor before we get a cut. Those who like Orbital and John Woo know that more *is* more, that repetition is part of a cumulative dynamic." In his note accompanying a still from *Hard Boiled*, Jacobs relates, "As Woo's films have demonstrated, with more bullets, and a faster firing-rate, the gunfire spectacle can be ceaselessly extended."

"Tellurion": A dictionary definition: an apparatus for showing the manner in which the diurnal rotation and annual revolution of the earth and the obliquity of its axis produce the alternations of day and night and the changes of the season.

"Coole Jerk" unites these sources: W. B. Yeats, William Meredith, the 1966 pop song by the Capitols, and the 1990s cover version by the Go-Go's.

"Of *Dicebas quondam solum te nosse . . .*": The first name of Catullus is Gaius. Roy Arthur Swanson translates this poem:

> Catullus you once called your only love,
>   preferred to Jove, my Lesbia.
> I loved you, not as men love mistresses,
>   but as a father loves his heirs.
> I know you now: it makes my love more hot,
>   but you're more cheap, mere trash to me.
> "How so?" you ask. Such dirt heaps up my love
>   but buries all my friendliness.

"Four Days": *Maria Callas* by Jürgen Kestling, translated by John Hunt.

"Pretext": An entry in *The Encyclopedia of Unusual Sex Practices* by Brenda Love explains that "furtling (furtivus: stolen or hidden) refers to the once popular entertainment of manipulating one's hand underneath a photo that had a small area cut out where the legs, breasts or genitals were located. Placing one's hand behind this space gave the illusion of seeing real life genitals or buttocks. Burton Silver and Jeremy Bennett have written a book (*The Naughty Victorian Hand Book, Furtling: The Rediscovered Art of Erotic Hand Manipulation*) that contains examples of this erotic art form with a history of its appeal and demise under Victorian influence." Love goes on to clarify that "the reason the word furtling is used is because the sketches are all of normal people who are unknowingly or unintentionally exposing themselves to others; such as a woman watching a male nude swimmer towel dry through a telescope, or a woman who just had the front of her skirt bitten out by a horse, exposing her genitals. There are hands drawn on each previous page giving instructions on exactly how to hold the fingers behind the hole."

"He Is Our Greatest Poet of Blood": A line by André Malraux from *Saturn, An Essay on Goya*, translated by C. W. Chilton.